To Rachel – from her mother –
Virginia Isaacs

ISBN 1-58660-435-X

Cover art © Photodisc, Inc.

Viola Ruelke Gommer contributed to the selections on pages 9, 14, 19, 20, 26, and 35.

Published by Barbour Books, an imprint of Barbour Publishing, Inc.,
P.O. Box 719, Uhrichsville, Ohio 44683
www.barbourbooks.com

Member of the
Evangelical Christian
Publishers Association

Printed in China.

LIFTING YOU IN PRAYER

ELLYN SANNA

HIS ears are open
to their prayers.

1 PETER 3:12 NLT

I'M LIFTING YOU IN PRAYER...

when your burdens are heavy
and when you walk through fire.

And I'm praying. . .

that you'll receive God's grace from above,
and know His presence is at your side.

Please know you are not alone.
Love supports you, and prayer joins us together.

WE can be confident that he will listen to us
whenever we ask him for anything in line with his will.
And if we know he is listening when we make our requests,
we can be sure that he will give us what we ask for.

1 JOHN 5:14–15 NLT

1

WHEN YOUR BURDENS ARE HEAVY

*Cast your burden on the LORD,
and he will sustain you.*

PSALM 55:22 NRSV

I'M praying that God will lighten the burden you carry.
May His loving hand wash the pain from your heart.
May He dry your tears. . .
that you might see more clearly
His purpose for your life.

I pray that the fears you carry
will nudge you through the door of courage.
I pray that these burdensome times will be transformed;
that you will find new privileges of grace,
new challenges and opportunities,
new growth.

WE HAVE INHERITED NEW DIFFICULTIES BECAUSE WE HAVE INHERITED NEW PRIVILEGES.

ABRAM SACHER

When life weighs so heavy that
you're left gasping for breath,
I'm praying you will open
the windows of your life
And breathe in the Holy Spirit.

AS wise women and men in every culture tell us:
The art of life is not controlling what happens to us,
but using what happens to us.

GLORIA STEINEM

DIFFICULTIES STRENGTHEN THE MIND, AS LABOR DOES THE BODY.

SENECA

THE man who removed mountains
began by carrying away small stones.

CHINESE PROVERB

THIS alone is to be feared—
the closed mind, the sleeping imagination,
the death of the spirit.

WINIFRED HOLTBY

PAIN IS LIFE—THE SHARPER, THE MORE EVIDENCE OF LIFE.

CHARLES LAMB

PAIN and pleasure, light and darkness,
succeed each other.

LAURENCE STERNE

I WILL SATISFY THE WEARY, AND ALL WHO ARE FAINT I WILL REPLENISH.

JEREMIAH 31:25 NRSV

I see the load you're carrying.
I can sense how difficult it is for you
to keep going beneath its weight.
Depend on Christ's strength instead of your own.
He who carried the cross
can also carry this heavy burden of yours.
Do not despair.
I am lifting you in prayer.

THE fact that God has prohibited despair
gives misfortune the right to hope all things,
and leaves hope free to dare all things.

ANNIE SOPHIE SWETCHINE

HOPE IS THE PARENT OF FAITH.

CYRUS A. BARTOL

THE joy the Lord gives you
will make you strong.

NEHEMIAH 8:10 TEV

I PRAY TODAY THAT YOUR FAITH
WILL BE STRENGTHENED. . .
AND YOUR HOPES FOR TOMORROW
WILL BECOME REALITY.

MAY God's love, mercy, and peace
comfort you and support you
today and in the days ahead.

2

WHEN YOU WALK THROUGH FIRE

When you walk through fire you shall not be burned,
and the flame shall not consume you.

ISAIAH 43:2 NRSV

FIRE IS THE TEST OF GOLD, ADVERSITY OF STRONG MEN.

SENECA

When we're walking through fire, we fear we will be consumed. We suspect our life is going up in smoke and nothing will be left but cinders and ashes.

But like the three Israelite men in the furnaces of Nebuchadnezzar, we are not alone in the fire. Someone has joined us in the flames—the Son of God—and He will keep the flames from singeing even the hair on our heads. When our walk through the flames is over, we won't even smell like smoke.

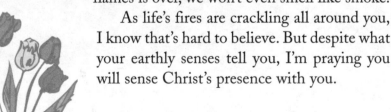

As life's fires are crackling all around you, I know that's hard to believe. But despite what your earthly senses tell you, I'm praying you will sense Christ's presence with you.

THEY saw that the fire had not harmed their bodies,
nor was a hair of their heads singed;
their robes were not scorched,
and there was no smell of fire on them

DANIEL 3:27 NIV

STRANGE and mighty things happen when we trust in God.
God did not neglect the three Israelite men
in their hour of need.
He brought them the comfort of
His protection and presence.
And He will not fail us either.

ELDYN SIMONS

THE one thing more than anything else that I wish for you is to discover that you are not alone, and that the stranger in the fire with you is God. That discovery is the discovery of God in your life and work, and I could wish no greater discovery for you—here and now—than that, and when you have discovered that, you have discovered everything.

PETER J. GOMES

IN THE WORLD YOU WILL HAVE TRIBULATION;
BUT BE OF GOOD CHEER,
I HAVE OVERCOME THE WORLD.

JOHN 16:33 NKJV

IN the midst of this hard time,
I pray that you will not withdraw from life.
May you not wrap the blanket of resentment around your heart.
I pray you don't give in to bitterness and despair.
This is only one hard experience in your life's journey.
Soon God will send you something new;
He'll open a path that leads straight through the fire.

HIS DIVINE POWER HAS GIVEN US
EVERYTHING NEEDED FOR LIFE.

2 PETER 1:3 NRSV

MY FLESH AND MY HEART FAILETH: BUT GOD IS THE STRENGTH OF MY HEART, AND MY PORTION FOR EVER.

PSALM 73:26 KJV

God waters the flames of adversity with His love.
Even now, in the midst of this hard time,
He can give you a new heart filled with His joy.
He's promised you the best He has to offer:
Joy,
Hope,
Peace.
I'm praying that you'll see
the reality of His promises.
Get ready for a brand-new journey of faith!

3

GRACE FROM ABOVE

God says to you, "My grace is all you need."

2 CORINTHIANS 12:9 TEV

GOD revealed himself. . .
with all the suddenness of a flash of lightning,
showing. . .that He pervaded the universe
and that there was no place where God was not.

SOJOURNER TRUTH

Grace is a little like lightning—it flashes from heaven in an unex-
pected burst of light. It gives us a startling new glimpse of our
surroundings. In its sudden light we see a new truth, something
we didn't suspect—that God is all around us. We did nothing to
earn His presence; we do not deserve His love. Grace is His free
gift to us.

I'M PRAYING THAT YOUR LIFE WILL BE LIT
WITH FLASHES OF GRACE.

IT IS THE NATURE OF GRACE
ALWAYS TO FILL SPACES THAT HAVE BEEN LEFT EMPTY.

GOETHE

YOUR life may seem empty right now.
You may feel that everything you loved best
has been taken from you.
Everywhere you turn,
you encounter aching holes in your heart.
But those are the very spots where
God will pour His grace.

HOLY GROUND IS NOT A PLACE OF PILGRIMAGE: IT IS WHERE YOU ARE WHEN GOD FINDS YOU.

PETER J. GOMES

God's grace finds us in the midst of our darkest nights. It reaches into our loneliest, most dismal days. In the midst of our tears while we're lying sleepless in bed, while we're driving to work, while we're mindlessly performing some dreary chore. . .everywhere and anywhere grace touches us. And when it does, suddenly we find that ordinary linoleum or city pavement is transformed. We are standing on holy ground.

IT may not seem that way to you, I know. . .
but the ground on which
you walk today is holy too.
God's grace will never lose you.

4

GOD'S PRESENCE AT YOUR SIDE

When you pass through the waters,
I will be with you.

Isaiah 43:2 NRSV

Dear friend,

God made you,
God loves you,
and God will care for you, even now.
He knows your name and He's calling to you.
You belong to Him.
I pray you will feel His presence at your side.

BUT now says the LORD, he who created you. . .
he who formed you. . .
Do not fear, for I have redeemed you;
I have called you by name,
you are mine.

ISAIAH 43:1 NRSV

THE LORD IS FAR FROM THE WICKED,
BUT HE HEARS THE PRAYER
OF THE RIGHTEOUS.

PROVERBS 15:29 NRSV

THE LORD WILL BE YOUR CONFIDENCE
AND WILL KEEP YOUR FOOT FROM BEING CAUGHT.

PROVERBS 3:26 NRSV

WHEN the road ahead seems rocky and full of holes;
when you seem to stub your toe each time you take a step;
when you fear you will trip and fall,
and that one day you will be too tired to get back up. . .
remember:
you have an invisible Companion
who will never leave your side.

YOU cannot see Him.
You cannot always sense His presence.
Sometimes you feel so all alone.
But He is more real than all the heartaches in your life.
And if you should fall, His love will bear you up.

I BELIEVE IN HEARING THE INAUDIBLE
AND TOUCHING THE INTANGIBLE
AND SEEING THE INVISIBLE.

ADAM CLAYTON POWELL, JR.

GOD ENTERS BY A PRIVATE DOOR
INTO EVERY INDIVIDUAL.

RALPH WALDO EMERSON

GOD. . .is everywhere present.
He is not an occasional visitor,
nor ever more truly present than at this very moment.
He is always ready to flow into our heart;
indeed He is there now—
it is we who are absent.

ARTHUR FOOTE

SPIRITUALITY. . .is, quite simply, a way of life
that reveals an awareness of the sacred
and a relationship with the Holy One
in the midst of human frailty, brokenness, and limitations.

EDWARD C. SELLNER

I AM PRAYING THAT YOU WILL KNOW
THE REALITY OF GOD'S PRESENCE IN YOUR LIFE.

NEVER forget that you are not alone.
God is with you, helping and guiding.
He is the companion who never fails,
the friend whose love comforts and strengthens.
Have faith and He will do everything for you.

AUROBINDO

5

UNITED IN PRAYER

The prayer of the righteous is powerful and effective.

JAMES 5:16 NRSV

CERTAIN THOUGHTS ARE PRAYERS.
THESE ARE MOMENTS WHEN,
WHATEVER BE THE ATTITUDE OF THE BODY,
THE SOUL IS ON ITS KNEES.

VICTOR HUGO

WHETHER I'm spending time in prayer,
or simply going about my day,
my thoughts are always with you.
I know that loneliness is
so often the companion of pain and suffering.
But you are not alone.
God's arms of love are around you,
and He is only a prayer away.
And through prayer, I'm with you, too.

BE JOYFUL IN HOPE,
PATIENT IN AFFLICTION,
FAITHFUL IN PRAYER.

ROMANS 12:12 NIV

Dear Lord,
I pray today
that You would preserve my loved ones' spirits.
Strengthen her feet as she walks out her faith.
Displace his despair with hope.
Touch their days
with Your hope,
Your patience,
and most of all
Your faithful love.
Amen.

> ## Every man prays in his own language, and there is no language that God does not understand.
>
> DUKE ELLINGTON

Some mornings I spend time alone with God, a space set aside in my day just for prayer.

And I always pray for you.

Other days are so busy that it's all I can do to get up and on my way. I pray in snatches throughout the day: in the car, while I'm picking up the house, before I eat, as I fall asleep.

And I always pray for you.

> ## The fewer the words the better the prayer.
>
> MARTIN LUTHER

BEAR ONE ANOTHER'S BURDENS,
AND IN THIS WAY YOU WILL FULFILL THE LAW OF CHRIST.

GALATIANS 6:2 NRSV

YOU do not carry this burden alone.
Let some of the weight fall on my shoulders,
and I will join you in prayer
to the God who loves us both.

THE LORD'S PRAYER

Our Father in heaven,
may your name be honored.
May your kingdom come soon.
May your will be done here on earth,
just as it is in heaven.
Give us our food for today,
and forgive us our sins,
just as we have forgiven those
who have sinned against us.
And don't let us yield to temptation,
but deliver us from the evil one.

MATTHEW 6:9–13 NLT

WE OUGHT TO ACT WITH GOD
IN THE GREATEST SIMPLICITY,
SPEAKING TO HIM FRANKLY AND PLAINLY,
AND IMPLORING HIS ASSISTANCE
IN OUR AFFAIRS,
JUST AS THEY HAPPEN.

BROTHER LAWRENCE

As I lift you up in prayer,
I imagine myself placing you
and the circumstances of your life
in God's outstretched fingers.
You have nothing to fear.
I know you're in good hands!